QUILTS

Pennsylvania Wreath, 1890s

QUILTS

a charm book

Ljiljana Baird

Quilters' Resource publications

This edition first published in 1999 for
Quilters' Resource Inc.
P.O. Box 148850
Chicago, IL 60614
Phone (773) 278-5695

Copyright ©1999 MQ Publications Ltd

ISBN: 1 889682 136

Printed and bound in Italy

CONTENTS

Introduction 6

Patchwork 12

Appliqué 144

Index 253

Introduction

Appreciation of antique quilts has grown over the past several decades. From their humble origins as mere bedspreads, quilts now grace museum walls and fetch impressive prices in auction rooms. After languishing for more than a century in dusty attics, these priceless heirlooms are now recognized for their beauty, graphic sophistication, and outstanding craftsmanship.

A quilt is simply two layers of material with padding between, held together with stitches. The quilt top is traditionally decorative, either appliquéed (a design created by adding layers of fabric on top of one another) or constructed of pieces of cloth sewn together.

The technique for making quilted cloth goes back to the Egyptians and was introduced into Europe at the end of the eleventh century by the Crusaders, returning from the Holy Wars. They had adopted the Eastern style of quilted fabric

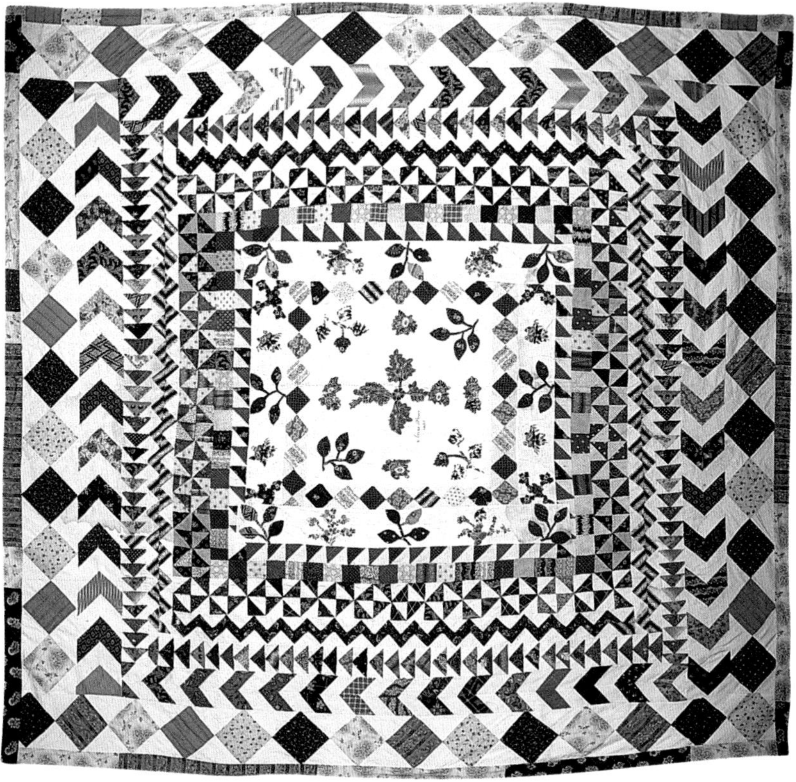

Anne Price, 1835

armory. Worn under metal armor it provided cushioning and protection from the rough metalwork, while for the poorer soldier it was a cheap and lightweight form of armor. As bed-coverings, quilts date back to the fourteenth century. Although there are earlier references to quilts in literature, wills, and household inventories, the earliest existing examples are a pair made in Sicily for the marriage of members of the Guicciardini and Acciaiuili families in 1395. Made of linen with wool lining, they have been quilted in brown linen thread with scenes from the life of Tristram.

In the following centuries both quilted garments and quilted bedcovers became increasingly popular and appear frequently in inventories of wealthy households. In 1592 Carew Castle in Wales lists:

> "Item ij(6) old quiltes of yellow sernet, xxs.
> Item a changeable silke quilt, price xxs.
> Item an old black and white silke quilt for a bedd, price iijs"

—and Catherine Howard, fifth wife of Henry VIII, was given twenty-three quilts as a mark of favor in 1540.

The arrival in Britain in the seventeenth century of colorful and colorfast glazed cotton chintzes from India had a remarkable impact on the popularity of quiltmaking. These polished Indian cottons featured large birds and exotic plants, and with these new motifs the emphasis in needlework moved from decorative quilting patterns to the application of figurative chintz motifs onto a solid ground. This technique became known as broderie perse.

After the seventeenth century the story of quiltmaking shifts to America. The tradition arrived with the early British settlers. In a very short time the disparate ethnic groups had adopted quiltmaking as their primary form of bedding for everyday use and for "best".

The first quilts made in America were modelled on the whole-cloth and medallion styles (a quilt with a central panel surrounded by a series of borders). A third early eighteenth-

New York Beauty, 1930

century quiltmaking option consisted of four large blocks, roughly 36 inches square, to which a wide border was added. It is from this model that the block quilt, as we know it today, emerged. Whether for portability, economy or ease of working smaller units, nineteenth-century quiltmakers experimented with progressively smaller blocks. This functional technique, developed in America in the early 1800s, became the quiltmaker's favorite method of quilt construction, and gave rise to the hundreds of new block patterns.

The one hundred and twenty quilts featured in this book represent just a tantalizing glimpse of the extraordinary world of quiltmaking. It is a treasure house of outstanding quilts from a remarkable textile heritage.

PATCHWORK

Basket with Eight-point Star

c. 1890
USA
167.6 x 203.2 cm / 66 x 80 in
PRIVATE COLLECTION

Baskets have always been a popular folk art motif. This charming quilt uses a symmetrical combination of both baskets and stars, making it a romantic interpretation of a traditional pattern.

The idea of "art" became a popular notion around this time and the widespread public confirmation of the "moral" value in art and design had two important effects on quilting. Firstly, it helped to reaffirm the woman's belief in her own creative handiwork. Secondly, the romanticism which permeated American culture encouraged the continuation of traditional quilting techniques which existed alongside newer methods.

Mariner's Compass

c. 1860
New York State, USA
170 x 221cm / 67 x 87 in
PRIVATE COLLECTION

A circle with radiating points is an old quilt pattern, and is thought to have evolved from the wind roses found on compass points and sea charts. The earliest known quilts bearing this pattern are English and date back to the eighteenth century.

This elegant variation has been worked in a distinguished palette of brown, red, pink, white and green. using a lovely selection of nineteenth-century small print cotton fabrics. It is a challenging quilt design to construct because it requires extremely accurate cutting and piecing to ensure that the narrow and sharp points meet precisely.

17

Amish Diamond in a Square

c. 1930
Lancaster County, Pennsylvania, USA
198 x 198 cm / 78 x 78 in
PRIVATE COLLECTION

This abstract, geometric design with dramatic use of vivid and saturated color is the hallmark of modern art and a modern lifestyle. The same words aptly describe this typical Amish quilt, yet it was made by a community that shuns a modern lifestyle.

The Diamond in a Square is a popular Amish design—a square within a square. It is a development of the central medallion style of quilt, and its design simplicity illustrates the Amish pursuit of spiritual truth through a philosophy of simplicity. This fine wool quilt is a wonderful example of the awe-inspiring color preferences of the Amish quilters in Pennsylvania.

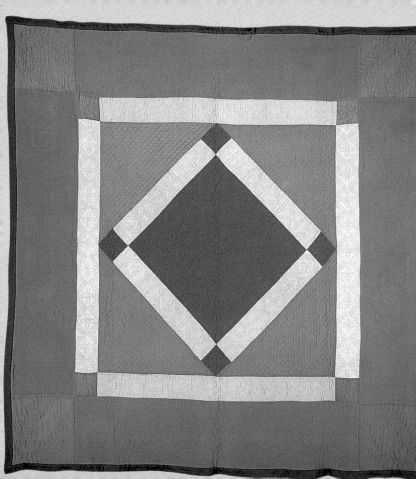

Ocean Waves

c. 1880
Ohio, USA
173 x 183 cm / 68 x 72 in
PRIVATE COLLECTION

Throughout the nineteenth century indigo-dyed blue and white was a popular color choice for both pieced and appliqué quilts, as well as woven coverlets.

Indigo was introduced to Europe in the mid-sixteenth century from India, and replaced the extremely difficult blue-dye technique using the plant woad. It remained in use as the main source of blue dye until 1856 when synthetic aniline dyes were invented.

This quilt is a challenging piecing exercise, and is a testimonial to the maker's sewing ability; several thousand, tiny one-inch triangles have been sewn together to create the dark grid that represents the ocean waves.

Early Nine-patch

early 1800s
USA
234 x 259 cm / 92 x 102 in
PRIVATE COLLECTION

The nine-patch design is a simple pattern, popular with novice and experienced quilters alike; for the novice because it is simple to cut and piece, and for the experienced because it is the basis of many and more difficult patterns.

Stars

1855

Texas, USA

223 x 238 cm / 88 x 94 in

PRIVATE COLLECTION

 The star pattern has been used repeatedly throughout the history of quiltmaking, and the possible variations are seemingly endless. It outnumbers all other patterns in popularity.

As well as representing a hopeful and romantic image, the star pattern also offers a needlework challenge. Most star patterns are constructed from diamond-shaped pieces. Cutting and sewing these acute angles with precision requires great skill. Like a jigsaw puzzle all the pieces must fit precisely together, any variation will throw the whole pattern out. Countless *Lone Star* quilt tops exist, unfinished because of an error.

Underground Railroad

c. 1870
USA
229 x 229 cm / 90 x 90 in
PRIVATE COLLECTION

The resonance of the bitter debate on slavery is felt in the naming of this quilt. The "underground railway" was an organization of individuals who helped spirit slaves to safety in the North and in Canada.

This two-color quilt is a simple nine-patch construction of thirty-six blocks. However, the finished appearance is one of considerable complexity. The strong diagonal thrust dominates its square construction and requires the viewer's concentration to "see" the nine-patch block.

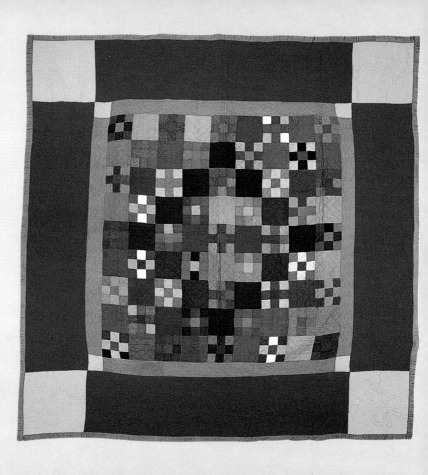

Amish Nine-patch

c. 1920
Lancaster County, Pennsylvania, USA
206 x 208 cm / 81 x 82 in
PRIVATE COLLECTION

 This masterful nine-patch suggestively places solid black blocks within the central square, subtly echoing the Lancaster County fondness for the *Diamond in the Square* pattern. In contrast to the geometric piecing the quilting is an intricate pattern of vines, wreaths, and clusters of grapes. The glowing quality of this piece may be attributed to the saturated color woolens as well as to a cloth used by the Amish of this period—Henrietta cloth—with its silk warp and wool weft.

Dove at the Window

c. 1880

Western Pennsylvania, USA

203 x 239 cm / 80 x 94 in

PRIVATE COLLECTION

The origin of this highly evocative pattern name is unknown. It conjures pictures of hope brought by the morning sun at the window; of the arrival of peace or simply of a bird flapping on the small panes of leaded glass. The theme of birds continues in the *Flying Geese* border and perhaps this quilt was inspired by the amazing sight of birds on migration.

Names for quilt patterns draw inspiration from any number of sources—nature, politics, events, daily life, folk motifs. Until the nineteenth century, pattern names were not documented and were passed orally from one quiltmaker to the next. In time, their origins were distorted, lost or re-invented to suit the maker.

Mennonite Joseph's Coat

c. 1920

Pennsylvania, USA

178 x 198 cm / 70 x 78 in

PRIVATE COLLECTION

This strikingly simple, geometric pattern is a variation of the Bars design. Whether inspired by the ploughed furrows or the neat rows of vegetable beds tended by a rural community, this pattern is a particular favorite of Mennonite, as well as Welsh and Amish quilters. The Welsh and the Amish usually translated the design as vertical bars.

Inspired by the Biblical story about Joseph and his coat of many colors, this quilt is a visual feast of color and quilting patterns. Pieced in narrow columns of plain cotton fabric, each of the seven different colored columns has been quilted with a different pattern – chains, diamonds, cable, zigzag, feather and a meandering Greek pattern.

Amish Bear's Paw

c. 1920
Ohio, USA
182.9 x 208.3 cm / 72 x 82 in

PRIVATE COLLECTION

 Bright colors on dark grounds characterize much of the work of Ohio Amish quilters. This inspired piece is beautifully proportioned and finely quilted.

Bear's Paw is the traditional name for several patterns worked by quilters in western Pennsylvania and Ohio, where bear tracks were a common sight. The same basic pattern also goes by the names *Duck's Foot in the Mud*, *Hands of Friendship* and *Hands All Around*.

Tree of Life

c. 1911
Blue Ridge Mountains, North Carolina, USA
157.5 x 188 cm / 62 x 74 in
PRIVATE COLLECTION

 The tree is a popular motif in quiltmaking, and first appears on eighteenth-century chintz cut-out appliqué (broderie perse) quilts. The decorative flowering tree offered a sense of domestic comfort in what was, for many, a great and frightening wilderness. By the nineteenth century settlers faced the natural world with confidence. They had domesticated the massive white pine that once filled their forefathers with awe and longing for the neat woods of Europe. It provided them with life-sustaining materials—timber for their log cabins and fuel for their fire, as well as furniture, cutlery, turpentine, paint and tar.

Other variations on the triangular-shaped tree are *Tree of Temptation*, *Temperance Tree*, and *Pine Tree*.

37

Charles Lindbergh Commemorative Quilt

1930

USA

193 x 211cm / 76 x 83 in

PRIVATE COLLECTION

The rush of technological achievement in the twentieth century was cause for celebration, and from the excitement, a host of new quilt patterns emerged.

The solo flight of Charles Lindbergh across the Atlantic in 1927 in the Spirit of St Louis airplane, caught the popular imagination, and commercial pattern makers were quick to produce this design. Twenty-one single engine airplanes in white calico on a saffron yellow ground have been simply pieced and finished with an appliquéed propeller.

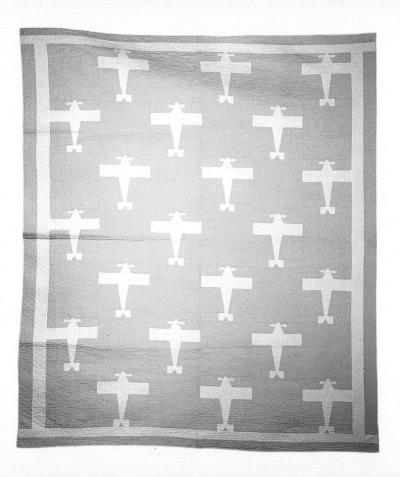

Medallion Sampler

c. 1850
Pennsylvania, USA
213 x 213 cm / 84 x 84 in
COURTESY ALY GOODWIN

 A sampler quilt is often made as a teaching or learning quilt. Here a novice quilter may practice his or her skills on a variety of different piecing and appliqué patterns. For the experienced quiltmaker they offer an opportunity to experiment with different blocks and techniques without committing the time needed to make a large quilt.

In this early and unusual sampler, twenty-eight blocks have been sewn onto a foundation cloth. The sun, made up from many radiating bands of small triangles and the four tulip pots have been appliquéed directly onto the foundation.

Shoo-fly

c. 1860

USA

183 x 183 cm / 72 x 72 in

PRIVATE COLLECTION

"Flies in the buttermilk shoo, fly, shoo
Flies in the buttermilk shoo, fly, shoo
Flies in the buttermilk shoo, fly, shoo
Skip to my Lou my darling."

This quilt teams with vitality – like a swarm of flies around the milk pot. The name is also associated with the famous Shoo-fly pie: a gooey, spiced cake baked with molasses in a flaky pastry, which being so sweet attracts flies during the baking.

The shoo-fly block is a simple nine-patch design, and in this variation the four corner blocks have been cut in half to make triangles. giving the block its busy appearance.

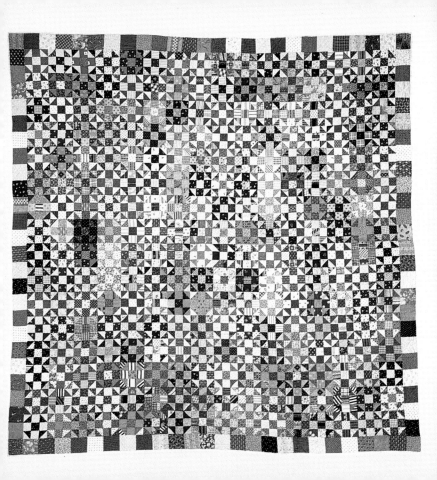

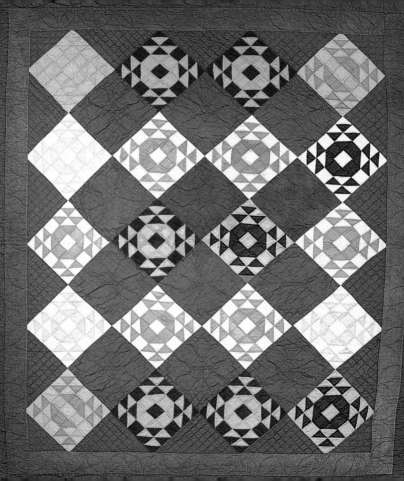

Amish Crown of Thorns

c. 1920
Iowa, USA
183 x 183 cm / 72 x 72 in
PRIVATE COLLECTION

 Although deeply devout, the Amish quilter used few patterns with an obvious religious connection. The *Crown of Thorns* is a rare exception to this rule. Many Amish quilt patterns may have specific pictorial names but they are pieced using abstract geometric shapes because pictorial realism in a quilt top is forbidden by the Amish church. This pattern is a simple construction which artfully employs triangles and squares.

Young Man's Fancy

c. 1900
New England, USA
140 x 178 cm / 55 x 70 in
PRIVATE COLLECTION

Before 1810 this complex variation of a nine-patch pattern was humorously called *Goose on the Pond*. Almost 1000 cotton fabric squares and triangles have been cut and pieced together to make this handsome quilt, each block requiring seventy-three separate pieces.

The quilt is reminiscent of a style popular in the early part of the nineteenth century. Freedom quilts were made by friends and family for a young man to celebrate the event of reaching twenty-one years. The quilt was usually put away until his engagement, at which time it was presented to his future bride.

Log Cabin, Pineapple Variation

c. 1870
Kentucky, USA
178 x 178 cm / 70 x 70 in
PRIVATE COLLECTION

 The *Log Cabin* as a quilt pattern name is mentioned in literature of the 1860s and, may have been inspired by Abraham Lincoln's presidential campaign of 1862. The Pineapple variation of the *Log Cabin* design is an extremely complicated pattern. The juxtaposition of light and dark shapes in this challenging quilt moves your eye through a series of changing patterns from four-pointed stars, to interlocking circles, bull's-eyes, and windmill sails. Made from lengths of old woollen cloth, this mesmerizing quilt is an outstanding example of the design inventiveness of quilters.

Spools

c. 1890
Kansas, USA
152 x 188 cm / 60 x 74 in
PRIVATE COLLECTION

 Spools is a popular nineteenth-century scrap pattern and its name must lie close to the heart of any active needleperson.

It would have taken the maker a long time to accumulate enough fabric remnants to make up the 2300 pieces needed for this quilt.

Quiltmakers spend many years collecting fabric scraps and in the nineteenth century when women of every age, class and race sewed, scrap bags would have been common to all households. In it went leftover dress and furnishing fabrics as well as worn garments. Women exchanged their scraps and passed on their valuable collection to their children and grandchildren.

Military Patchwork

c. 1870

England

182 x 193 cm / 72 x 76 in

PRIVATE COLLECTION

Generally speaking, quiltmaking has been, and continues to be, a female activity. Men may have assisted in the art—by cutting fabric or designing and building quilting frames—but they have rarely participated in the actual piecing or quilting. From the large numbers of similar patchwork quilts made by the soldiers exhibited for the 1890 Royal Military Exhibition at the Chelsea Hospial in London, it can be safely assumed that this amazing mosaic quilt was worked by a man. Thousands of half-inch woolen squares, cut from regimental uniforms, have been pierced together in a variety of configurations to make up the twenty-five blocks. They are contained within a frame of smaller squares and finished with a zigzag border.

Grandmother's Flower Garden

made by Dena Williams
c. 1930
Wright City, Missouri, USA
183 x 244 cm / 72 x 96 in
PRIVATE COLLECTION

Grandmother's Flower Garden, Dresden Plate and *Double Wedding Ring* were the most popular patterns of the early twentieth century.

It is a one-patch design constructed from hexagon shapes, which emerge as a honeycomb when sewn together. Joining the hexagons into rings was a way of making the sewing more manageable.

To create the garden, a mid-toned hexagon is used for the center. This is then surrounded by one or more rings of flower-colored prints, a ring of green for the foliage and a ring of white to represent the path.

Log Cabin, Light and Dark Variation

c. 1880
Kentucky, USA
178 x 208 cm / 70 x 82 in
PRIVATE COLLECTION

 The name of this type of quilt refers to its log-like contruction. Narrow strips of cloth are assembled onto a foundation cloth in the same way that logs are layered in the building of a cabin. The pattern is built up around a small central square, usually red, and which supposedly represents the hearth. The placement of light and dark strips within each block and the arrangement of the blocks creates the overall pattern. There are at least six different variations of the Log Cabin design—*Court House Steps*, *Barn Raising*, *Streak of Lightning*, *Straight Furrows*, and *Pineapple*.

Flowerpots

c.1880

Pennsylvania USA

101.6 x 104.1 cm / 40 x 41 in

COURTESY MARTHA JACKSON COLLECTION

 The basket shape, whether appliquéed like the elaborate, flower filled baskets of the Baltimore Album quilts or pieced into a simple, geometric shape remains a popular quilt pattern.

When the fashion for appliqué quilts was replaced by quilts made using the block-constructed method, the basket shape was adapted and simplified into various geometric configurations. The patterns, *Flower Pot*, *Basket of Chips*, *Cake Stand* and *Grape Basket* are all pieced using a different arrangement of small and large triangles.

This quilt uses a popular mid-nineteenth-century color scheme of chrome yellow set against a dark indigo background.

New York Beauty

c. 1920
Michigan, USA
244 x 203 cm / 96 x 80 in
PRIVATE COLLECTION

 Quilt pattern names are numerous and changeable, and frequently are influenced by the environment and circumstance of the maker. For instance, this pattern was known in the nineteenth century as *Rocky Mountain Road* and *Crown of Thorns*, reflecting a time when life was hard and hazardous for early settlers, and religion provided them a source of comfort. The name *New York Beauty* is resonant with the buoyancy of the twentieth century and the new and prosperous quilt industry.

This magnificant quilt dazzles the eye with vibrant color and remarkably accurate stitching. The sawtooth blocks, sashing, and circular appliqué combine to make this a technical masterpiece.

Silk Tumbling Blocks

c. 1870

USA

188 x 191 cm / 74 x 75 in

PRIVATE COLLECTION

 Sketchy provenance on this quilt suggests that it was made out of ball gowns from a family in Louisville, Kentucky. It is a glorious array of patterned and plain silks and taffetas arranged as to achieve a three-dimensional illusion.

The Victorians were fascinated by optical illusion and incorporated some of the principles into their quiltmaking. Depending on how you view this quilt, the blocks change from appearing as an opened concertina of postcards to blocks that seem to radiate from the center of the quilt. It is a one-patch design, formed from three diamond-shaped pieces, rather than from squares. The illusion is achieved by the placement of light, medium, and dark colors.

Amish Log Cabin, Barn Raising Variation

c. 1900
Pennsylvania, USA
193 x 203 cm / 76 x 80 in
PRIVATE COLLECTION

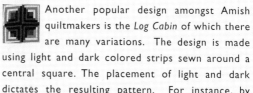 Another popular design amongst Amish quiltmakers is the *Log Cabin* of which there are many variations. The design is made using light and dark colored strips sewn around a central square. The placement of light and dark dictates the resulting pattern. For instance, by arranging the strips in diagonals of light and dark, you can create the *Barn Raising* and *Straight Furrows* patterns.

Yo-yo Quilt

1925

USA

157.5 x 213.4 cm / 62 x 84 in

PRIVATE COLLECTION

 The Yo-yo quilt is a modern novelty quilt that emerged at the time of the yo-yo craze. It was particularly popular during the period 1925–1950 and, like the *Cathedral Window* quilt, it was made as a decorative throw. It is not a quilt in the true sense of being made up of three layers and stitched together. The yo-yo is made entirely of small circles of cloth about three inches in diameter, the edges are turned in and gathered with thread and fastened, so that the medallion is smooth on one side and puckered on the other. The separate medallions are joined either in a specific design or in a random way reminiscent of scrap quilts.

Evergreen

c. 1920
Texas, USA
168 x 218 cm / 66 x 86 in
PRIVATE COLLECTION

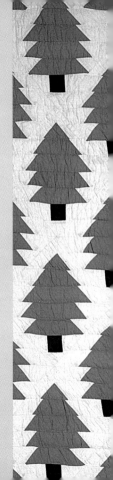

The tree, in all its varieties, has been a popular motif in American quiltmaking. This seasonal quilt, which expands our visual concept of Christmas, was made from a kit during the 1920s when commercially printed patterns encouraged quilters to embark on new and challenging projects. Commercial patterns meant that quilts were no longer exclusively one-of-a-kind, and they served to fuel a huge revival in quilting.

Victorian Crazy Crib Quilt

c. 1890

USA

46 x 61 cm / 18 x 24 in

PRIVATE COLLECTION

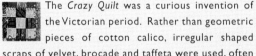 The *Crazy Quilt* was a curious invention of the Victorian period. Rather than geometric pieces of cotton calico, irregular shaped scraps of velvet, brocade and taffeta were used, often from worn out garments and furnishing fabrics. They are frequently very personal keepsakes containing stitched moments of someone's life. The national passion for Crazy Quilts was shortlived, yet the stylistic concept continued well after the turn of the century using more ordinary fabrics, such as dark woolens and heavy suiting materials.

This piece is unusual because it features a central medallion of an embroidered bouquet of daisies surrounded by a traditional nine-patch block.

Primitive Schoolhouses

c. 1880
Vermont, USA
152 x 178 cm / 60 x 70 in
PRIVATE COLLECTION

The one-room schoolhouse is a popular and symbolic motif in American culture. The quilt pattern was developed during the last half of the nineteenth century, and in the unsettled and dangerous world of the new frontier, it represented an achievement of stability and permanence.

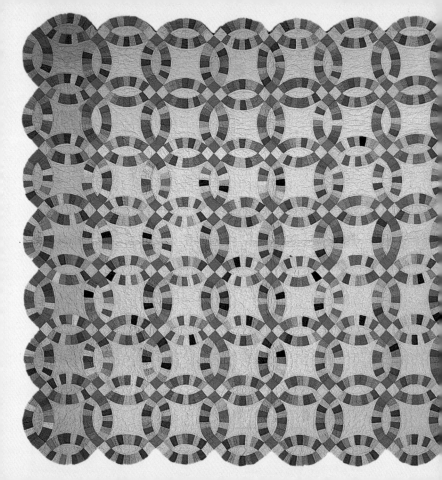

Double Wedding Ring

c. 1930
USA
183 x 208 cm / 72 x 82 in
PRIVATE COLLECTION

This challenging pattern of interlocking rings, thought originally to have been a German design, came to symbolize the bands of marriage and was often given as a wedding gift. It was introduced in the mid-nineteenth century and reached its height of popularity in the early twentieth century with the advent of pre-cut templates, which made this exacting quilt pattern very much easier to make.

Ohio Star

c. 1840
USA
193 x 229 cm / 76 x 90 in
PRIVATE COLLECTION

This stunning quilt, with its exciting combination of a rare copper-plate Regency pillar print in the border and plain blocks and Provençal inspired prints used to piece the Ohio star blocks, is a textile enthusiast's dream. Regency fabrics were strongly influenced by classical themes, hence the penchant for Greek and Roman columns. The star is one of the oldest and most popular quilt motifs and at least 100 variations can be identified.

Mennonite Baskets

c. 1880

Bloserville, Pennsylvania, USA
167.6 x 203.2 cm / 66 x 80 in
PRIVATE COLLECTION

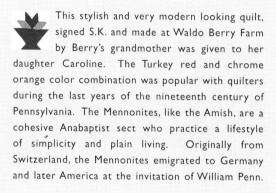 This stylish and very modern looking quilt, signed S.K. and made at Waldo Berry Farm by Berry's grandmother was given to her daughter Caroline. The Turkey red and chrome orange color combination was popular with quilters during the last years of the nineteenth century of Pennsylvania. The Mennonites, like the Amish, are a cohesive Anabaptist sect who practice a lifestyle of simplicity and plain living. Originally from Switzerland, the Mennonites emigrated to Germany and later America at the invitation of William Penn.

Amish Unknown Design

c. 1920
Mifflin County, Pennsylvania, USA
170 x 183 cm / 67 x 72 in
PRIVATE COLLECTION

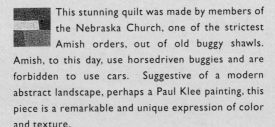This stunning quilt was made by members of the Nebraska Church, one of the strictest Amish orders, out of old buggy shawls. Amish, to this day, use horsedriven buggies and are forbidden to use cars. Suggestive of a modern abstract landscape, perhaps a Paul Klee painting, this piece is a remarkable and unique expression of color and texture.

Feathered Star in Blue and Gold

c. 1920

Kentucky, USA

193 x 198 cm / 76 x 78 in

PRIVATE COLLECTION

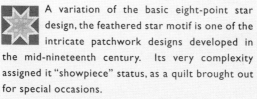 A variation of the basic eight-point star design, the feathered star motif is one of the intricate patchwork designs developed in the mid-nineteenth century. Its very complexity assigned it "showpiece" status, as a quilt brought out for special occasions.

This example in Wedgwood blue has been finished with a delicate sawtooth border that imitates the "feathering" of the internal blocks.

16-Patch on Point

c. 1860
Ohio, USA
229 x 244 cm / 90 x 96 in
PRIVATE COLLECTION

Interesting printed calicos, triple row quilting, and blocks set on point transform this otherwise simple pattern into a noteworthy quilt. Although it is often hard to discern regional styles, recent state quilt projects have unearthed new information which help to characterize particular trends. Setting blocks on point and diagonal rows of triple quilting are distinctive techniques discovered to have been popular with early Ohio quiltmakers.

North Carolina Lily

c. 1930
Missouri, USA
198 x 203 cm / 78 x 90 in
PRIVATE COLLECTION

 One of the best loved and most handsome patterns based on the lily, this pattern is often composed using a diamond-shaped block. It was an extremely popular design that migrated across the continent bearing a variety of names to suit new locales. Names included *Wood Lily*, *Mountain Lily*, *Fire Lily*, and *Meadow Lily*, among others. This charming example features an unusual appliqué vine border.

Seven Sisters

c. 1840

New England, USA

198 x 203 cm / 78 x 80 in

This unusual early quilt, with its considered sense of symmetry and color and wonderful collection of early fabrics, was rescued from the back seat of an old Chevy in St Louis. The design, which is rarely seen, takes its name from the Pleiades constellation of stars.

Flying Geese

c. 1880
USA
193 x 224 cm / 76 x 88 in
PRIVATE COLLECTION

The traditional *Flying Geese* pattern assembled in neat rows creates an elegant contrast to the flowing vine border which has been worked with decorative stuffed trapunto (see page 171) leaves and berries. The fabrics chosen for the triangles represent a beautiful selection of nineteenth-century madder-style dyed prints.

Amish Bars

c. 1930

Lancaster County, Pennsylvania, USA

179 x 203 cm / 70 x 80 in

PRIVATE COLLECTION

A traditional pattern in colors much favored by Lancaster County Amish quilters, this stunning quilt could pass for a work of twentieth-century art. The simple geometric design was used by early Amish quilters in a conscious effort to avoid emulating the decorative and pictorial quilts made by the majority of American women in the 1870s. The stark linear motif has been complemented by a fabulously intricate quilting pattern featuring wreaths and climbing vines.

Mennonite Starburst

c. 1920
Pennsylvania, USA
213.4 x 213.4 cm / 84 in x 84 in
PRIVATE COLLECTION

A unique application of the star motif, this inspired Mennonite quilt has elaborate patterns of feather, scroll, and wreath quilting on the solid blue background. The central pieced star is reminiscent of German motifs often found painted on Pennsylvania barns.

Rainbow Schoolhouses

c. 1940
USA
193 x 203 cm / 76 x 80 in
PRIVATE COLLECTION

The American one-room schoolhouse has long been a potent symbol of a community's stability and respectability, second only to the church. The schoolhouse pattern itself became a popular figurative motif at the end of the last century. This unusual example artfully employs rainbow-hued colors organized into diagonal bands, all of which are punctuated by bright pink stars.

Carpenter's Square

late nineteenth century
USA
151.8 x 191.1 cm / 60 x 75 in
PRIVATE COLLECTION

Sources of inspiration for many quilts are either domestic objects like cake stands and baskets or natural elements like flowers and birds. It is unusual to find a quilt which is directly named after a household tool. Another interesting feature of this late-nineteenth-century quilt is the curved machine quilting, a point which testifies to the growing pride which accompanied the ownership of a sewing machine.

Amish Sunshine and Shadow

c. 1920

Lancaster County, Pennsylvania, USA

96.5 x 96.5 cm / 38 x 38 in

PRIVATE COLLECTION

This inviting quilt was made for a child's cot. The color scheme, however, is not the typical pastel or primary shades of today's nursery, but the vibrant and saturated palette favored by Amish quilters. Reduced scale one-inch squares in rich blues, greens, and plums form concentric diamonds contained within a velvety black border.

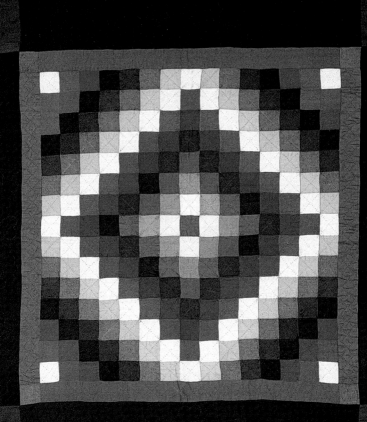

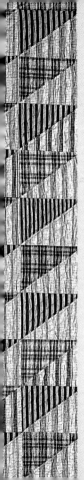

String of Flags

late nineteenth century
USA
182.9 x 223.5 cm / 72 x 88 in
PRIVATE COLLECTION

Made entirely of what appears to be patterned shirting material, this deceptively simple quilt is a simple variation on the ever-present triangle. The muted tonality of the quilt gives it both a "homey" and a sophisticated appearance.

Maple Leaf

c. 1880

Holmes County, Ohio, USA

167.6 x 182.9 cm / 66 x 72 in

PRIVATE COLLECTION

It is hard to imagine that this strikingly modern looking quilt was made by a Holmes County, Ohio, housewife around 1880. Chrome orange and Turkey red was a popular color combination during this period.

Zigzag Bricks

c. 1880
Missouri, USA
171.5 x 212cm / 67 x 83in
PRIVATE COLLECTION

Made in Missouri around 1880, this simple yet striking quilt displays a fascinating array of the small-scale and sober colored prints that were fashionable during the latter part of the nineteenth century. The quilt is constructed in rows and is the easiest quilt in the book to make.

Prairie Stars with Prairie Points

1880
Mid-West, USA
167.6 x 213.4 cm / 66 x 84 in
PRIVATE COLLECTION

 This quilt consists of Turkey red stars on a white background. It is an interesting variation with pieced eight-point stars in the corners of each star block. A decorative border of folded prairie points complements the fascinating graphic design.

Pyramids

c. 1900

USA

129.5 x 218.4 cm / 51 x 86 in

PRIVATE COLLECTION

This simple design is created by sewing bands of alternating colored and plain triangles. The name *Pyramids* refers to the triangle shape used: a short baseline triangle.

In this quilt of lush Victorian velvets, the black triangles vie for dominance with identically sized triangles pieced from narrow colorful strips. When the quilt is viewed vertically, the pattern appears as a zigzag basket weave. In a horizontal position, the black faced triangles appear three-dimensional, with the colored triangles providing the illusion of depth.

Snow Crystals

c. 1920

Oklahoma, USA

181.6 x 228.6 cm / 71 x 90 in

COURTESY VICTORIA WEIL

 Pattern names are often idiosyncratic and this one is perhaps no exception. This lovely quilt, made in Oklahoma during the 1920s, is a variation of the star design. The pattern was probably originally Arabic, and then spread to Europe with adaptations to Western culture. Blue and white have been the most popular quilt colors throughout the past century; this piece is particularly pleasing in that it subtly exploits two contrasting shades of blue. The twenty blocks are each given distinction by the darker blue sashing with center white posts.

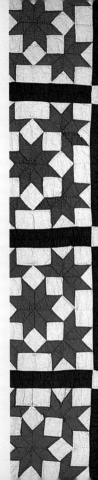

Birds in the Air

c. 1890
North Carolina, USA
182.9 × 213.4 cm / 72 × 84 in
PRIVATE COLLECTION

The light triangles which seem to flutter across the surface of this quilt are evocative of the flight of birds on their autumn migration—hence the name of this traditional patchwork pattern: *Birds in the Air*. It was made around 1890 in North Carolina and displays some of the characteristics of a traditional Appalachian quilt: a dark background fabric and rather large quilting stitches.

Double Irish Chain

c. 1880
Delaware County, Pennsylvania, USA
213.4 x 228.5 cm / 84 x 90 in
PRIVATE COLLECTION

The Irish Chain is a simple piecing pattern that has long been popular with novice quilters, and since the nineteenth century the design has been frequently used for making scrap and utility quilts. This quilt is pieced in Turkey red (a fashionable natural red dye of the period), green, and cream, and has been beautifully quilted and finished with an elegant border.

Drunkard's Path

1880s
Ohio, USA
203 x 188 cm / 80 x 74 in
PRIVATE COLLECTION

This early nineteenth-century pattern illustrates the wide diversity of names given to a single design. Other names for this particular pattern include *Solomon's Puzzle*, *Rocky Road to Dublin*, *Rocky Road to California*, *Country Cousin*, and *Robbing Peter to Pay Paul*. Technically, the pattern itself is simple but the particular arrangement of blocks with curved seams makes it a charming quilt. The lovely beige and red colors in this example, as well as the pieced border treatment, create an overall satisfying and harmonious quilt.

Missouri Folk Art Lily

1850s
Missouri, USA
162.5 x 208.3 cm / 64 x 82 in
PRIVATE COLLECTION

This is a unique design and reveals the high level of design sophistication achieved by many nineteenth-century quiltmakers. The complicated piecing arrangement of small interlocking triangles is testimony to the extraordinary technical skill of the maker.

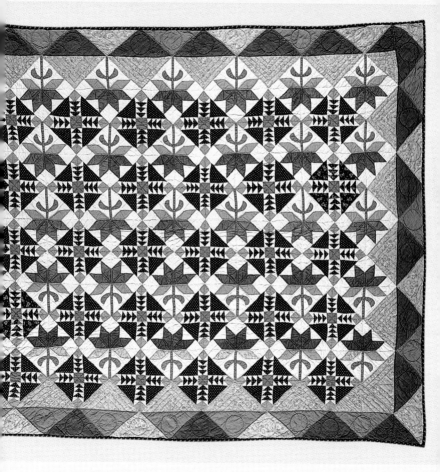

Mennonite Log Cabin, Barn Raising Variation

c. 1910

Quakertown, Pennsylvania, USA

190.5 x 190.5 cm / 75 x 75 in

PRIVATE COLLECTION

 Log Cabin designs date back to the 1840 presidential race when General William Harrison ran a "log cabin and cider barrel" election campaign. The log cabin represented the virtues attached to simple country living, an idea effectively used in 1862 in Abraham Lincoln's campaign. This graphic quilt is one of six variations of log cabin quilts, each of which employs a different arrangement of light and dark strips.

Log Cabin, Hap Quilt

1880s
Pennsylvania, USA
198 x 193 cm / 78 x 76 in
COURTESY GIDEON WEIL

This rugged looking *Log Cabin* style quilt has been made using a variety of what appears to be scraps of cotton shirts, suiting material and woolen fabrics. A Hap quilt is commonly known as a comforter.

Jane Austen Quilt

1811

Chawton, Hampshire, England

203.2 x 284.5 cm / 80 x112 in

This charming English quilt was made in 1811 by novelist Jane Austen, her sister Cassandra, and her mother at Chawton, where Jane spent her last eight years. In a letter to her sister, dated 1811, Jane enquires after the quilt, "Have you collected the pieces for the patchwork?" By the nineteenth century, quiltmaking was an established form of needlework amongst all classes of English society. The arrival of the colorful and colorfast chintz fabrics from India helped to popularize quiltmaking.

The Austen quilt is an unusual version of the medallion style—a diamond-shaped, chintz flower basket is surrounded by a pattern of repeating diamonds framed with a polka-dot print.

Poppyfield II

made by Pat Derrick
1993
Norfolk, England
58.4 x 68.5 cm / 23 x 27 in
COURTESY THE QUILTERS' GUILD OF
THE BRITISH ISLES

 Dozens of dazzling poppies seem ready to burst through the borders of this marvelous modern-day quilt. Indeed, Pat Derrick took her inspiration from the Norfolk poppyfields. The highly saturated colors have been carefully hand-dyed and help to give the variations of color that you find in nature.

Amish Lone Star

c. 1920
Texas, USA
208.3 x 223.5 cm / 82 x 88 in

Variously known as *Star of Bethlehem* and *Star of the East*, star quilts of this sort were generally brought out for Christmas. This mesmerising example is pieced point by point. Forty-eight diamonds of equal size are arranged in rows of different lengths to form the eight diamond-shaped points. The star is asymmetrically placed, allowing for an exceptionally beautiful detailed pillow panel. The coverlet is finished with the distinctive triangle and scallop edge border, a finishing technique popular between 1925 and 1950.

Union Army Encircled Star

c. 1860
USA
195.6 x 195.6 cm / 77 x 77 in
PRIVATE COLLECTION

It is said that this unique and highly complicated design quilt was made at a Quilting "Bee" for a fundraising auction supporting the Union Army. Pieced in the strong union colors of navy-blue and Cheddar yellow, this quilt is a celebration of the imaginative sense of design and extraordinary sewing skills that characterized much of nineteenth-century quilting in America.

Amish Broken Star

1940s
Ohio, USA
193 x 193 cm / 76 x 76 in
PRIVATE COLLECTION

The star is one of the earliest and most enduring quilt motifs and it has spawned countless variations. Stars are popular with Amish quilters as they are a celebration of the great firmament and God's grandeur, as well as requiring excellent sewing skills; a feature that has distinguished their community.

Black and White Optical Illusion

made by Maria Reuter
1980s
Germany
200 x 185 cm / 79 x 73 in
PRIVATE COLLECTION

From the mid-nineteenth century, optical illusion quilts have developed into an art form. With no formal training in geometry or color, some quilters choose to make quilts that challenge the normal perceptions of a simple bedcover, creating quilts that artistically preceded their generation by at least a hundred years.

Optical-illusion quilts cause the eye to see a three-dimensional shape while the mind recognises the flat surface of the quilt. By manipulating color, shape and line, by placing light and dark blocks in juxtaposition, quilters can create the illusions of third-dimension and movement.

Churn Dash

1930

USA

152.4 x 208.3 cm / 60 x 82 in

Like its namesake, this unevenly pieced quilt has a very rustic charm about it. And on inspection of seams and quilting stitches, we can suppose that it may have been the maker's first attempt at making a quilt. This traditional pattern in period printed textiles is composed of twenty-four-pieced blocks separated by blue printed sashing.

Flags

c. 1942

Arkansas, USA

193 x 218.4 cm / 76 x 86 in

COURTESY JOHN R. SAULS, TEXAS

For generations women have made quilts for fundraising purposes. During the two world wars many American women chose this way of "doing their bit" for their country and the boys abroad. In fact, thousands of dollars were raised through many such small efforts. This quilt, made by the Pleasant View House Demonstration Club and raffled at 10 cents a ticket, was won by Mr Kenny McAlister of the Baker Street Community.

Lone Star

1885

Wales

213.4 x 198.1 cm / 84 x 78 in

COURTESY RON SIMPSON

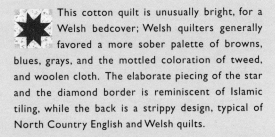 This cotton quilt is unusually bright, for a Welsh bedcover; Welsh quilters generally favored a more sober palette of browns, blues, grays, and the mottled coloration of tweed, and woolen cloth. The elaborate piecing of the star and the diamond border is reminiscent of Islamic tiling, while the back is a strippy design, typical of North Country English and Welsh quilts.

APPLIQUÉ

Coxcomb and Currant Variation

c. 1850

Peewee Valley, Kentucky, USA

191 x 203 cm / 75 x 80 in

PRIVATE COLLECTION

This exquisitely sewn, nineteenth-century quilt is a unique treatment of several very old piecing and appliqué patterns. The central intersecting pink and green cross is the *Wild Goose Chase* pattern. It is one of the earliest known patterns and dates back to the first half of the eighteenth century. The currants form a cruciform on top of the *Wild Goose Chase* and the showy coxcombs sweep across the composition like an oriental feathered fan.

The quilt has been executed in the favorite palette of nineteenth-century appliqué quiltmakers—red and green cottons with accents of bright pink and yellow. on a white background.

Alphabet Quilt

c. 1930

USA

178 x 229 cm / 70 x 90 in

PRIVATE COLLECTION

 Commercial pattern houses made a significant contribution to the twentieth-century quilt revival. The wealth of attractive and new patterns and, their easy availability through magazines, newspapers and mail order houses inspired many women to make quilts. The Nancy Page Quilt Club with the Publishers Syndicate, New York offered patterns for alphabet blocks weekly through the newspapers.

This highly amusing and individual alphabet quilt has only fifteen letters and the peculiar choice of words suggests that the maker was engaged in some game or word play with the three boys for whom it was made—Bruce, David and Steven, whose names are stitched on this quilt.

Centennial Eagle

c. 1876

Philadelphia, USA

178 x 223 cm / 70 x 88 in

PRIVATE COLLECTION

The Centennial celebrations in America produced a burst of creative energy on all levels of art, craft and needlework. Quilts with patriotic motifs abounded, and fabrics especially printed with flags, eagles, national heroes, prominent buildings and events were manufactured for quiltmakers.

This quilt, appliquéed in red and green on a white ground was made for the Exhibition. Its central motif is the Federal Eagle, flanked by two, diminutive songbirds. Ten wheels with spokes of carnation stems surround the three birds. There is a refreshing lack of uniformity to the appliqué pieces. They have been cut without a template—each carnation stem is different from the next, the central rosettes are of varying shape and size, and the saw-tooth border is as unique as any mountain range.

Album Quilt

1862

Pennington, New Jersey, USA

203 x 228.6 cm / 80 x 90 in

PRIVATE COLLECTION

 This remarkable quilt was made by members of the Ketcham family. Each block of the quilt is composed of different motifs, and several are inscribed in indelible ink with poems, sayings, and biblical references. The fabrics used are a combination of fine chintzes and glazed and plain cottons, often featuring intricate trapunto work. This stunning work testifies to the national penchant for documenting in quilts the close bonds which exisited among families and communities during the nineteenth century.

Sailors

c. 1940

USA

213 x 167 cm / 84 x 66 in

PRIVATE COLLECTION

 The twentieth century saw a proliferation of pieced and appliqué patterns inspired by everyday objects. While nineteenth-century quiltmakers abstracted reality into geometric patterns, the twentieth century sought a new realism. No object was too banal to immortalize in fabric—umbrellas, shoes, cups, cars, turtles, trolley cars, and donkeys. In the use of endless repetition of mundane objects, these light-hearted quilts can be seen as forerunners of the pop art movement.

Love and Luck

c. 1900
Vermont, USA
178 x 203 cm / 70 x 80 in
PRIVATE COLLECTION

This exuberant quilt in patriotic colors of red, blue and white was made using the paper-cutting method, popular amongst the Pennsylvanian German communities.

The fabric is folded to precise specifications and then cut so that a perfectly symmetrical pattern is formed. Using the heart as a single motif, the maker has cleverly arranged it to create a clover shape; no doubt following the old adage of where there is love there is luck. A careful and simple symmetry is achieved in the design by setting the large "clover" motif on point and surrounding it by smaller versions in a square formation.

158

Figurative Crazy Quilt

c. 1890

USA

218 x 185 cm / 86 x 73 in

COURTESY BETSY NIMOCK COLLECTION

 The Crazy quilt was a curious and fanciful Victorian invention. Rather than geometric pieces of cotton or wool, irregular shaped scraps of velvet, brocade, silk, satin, and taffeta were used. This splendid figurative crazy quilt is made up of twelve blocks; each is a rich and artful composition. They have been decorated with examples of the Victorian preoccupation for things new and exotic.

The idea of piecing together scraps of fabric dates back to the origins of patchwork when necessity dictated the random appearance of the finished item. But it is doubtful whether this utilitarian memory in any way influenced the extraordinary Crazy Quilt phenomenon that swept across America and England.

Whig's Defeat

c. 1860
Georgia, USA
229 x 236 cm / 90 x 93 in
COURTESY VICTORIA WEIL

 Quilt pattern names can provide us with an interesting record of public interest and feelings on any number of issues. From the political dispute during the 1840s between the Whigs and the Democrats two new quilt patterns emerged—the *Whig Rose* and the *Democrat Rose*, with each party claiming their own. The dispute was resolved at the 1844 elections with the defeat of the Whig presidential candidate, Henry Clay by the Democrat, James K. Polk. And from his demise sprang a new pattern name—*Whig's Defeat*.

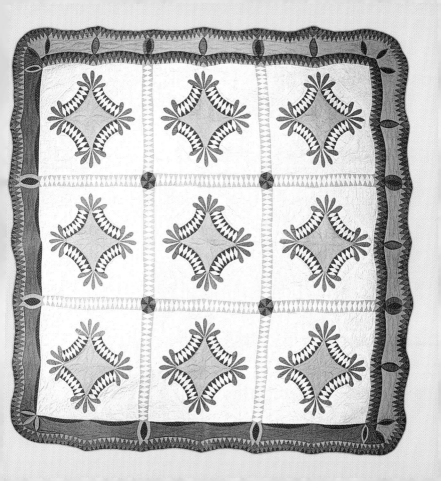

Princess Feather Variation

c. 1900

Skullkill County, Pennsylvania, USA

198 x 203 cm / 78 x 80 in

PRIVATE COLLECTION

 The feather as an appliqué pattern probably evolved around the nineteenth century and drew its inspiration from the feather quilting pattern. As a quilting pattern the feather motif dates back to the seventeenth century and there are many examples of it used in garments and coverlets.

The *Princess Feather*, of which there are many variations, is a large pattern demanding a lot of room. This version, worked in indigo blue and Turkey red on a white background, is composed of just four blocks. The slightly mismatched and irregularly-shaped feathers, stars, and tulips appear to have been cut without a template. In contrast, the quilt has been very evenly stitched in a precise cross-hatching pattern.

Mammy Quilt

signed and dated Lola 1902
USA
218 x 193 cm / 86 x 72 in
PRIVATE COLLECTION

 The mammy quilt was an unusual twentieth-century quilting phenomenon in which white needlewomen portrayed their perception of black characters. The prevailing attitude in the early part of the century was one of deep-seated racism, so it is not surprising that the characters portrayed were such stereotypes as Aunt Jemima, Little Black Boy, Sugar Pie, and Brown Koko.

Doll-like figures, each with a different, colorful frock and turban have been appliquéed by machine onto a ground of cinnamon pink. All look left, except the one in the bottom right-hand corner who alone looks right. The fabric for the frocks may have been cut from cotton dry-goods sacks. which were often packaged in cheap and cheerful printed cotton.

Pennsylvania Dutch Folk Art Appliqué

c. 1860

Pennsylvania, USA

183 x 233 cm / 72 x 92 in

PRIVATE COLLECTION

 Pennsylvania Dutch quilts are filled with joyful folk images and motifs, recalling memories of the new settlers' German-speaking home. Worked in lively colors of red, green, and yellow with abundant patches of brightly patterned calico, these quilts are a sign of the optimism that abounded among these settlers.

This mid-nineteenth-century quilt, incorporating appliqué, piecing, reverse appliqué, and embroidered cording on a green background, has the decorative qualities of the gingerbread house found by Hansel and Gretel. The oak leaf is the main motif, worked around the border and in the body of the quilt, evoking a picture of an ancient oak wood.

Floral Reverse Appliqué

c. 1870
Vermont, USA
132 x 218 cm / 82 x 86 cm
PRIVATE COLLECTION

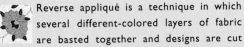Reverse appliqué is a technique in which several different-colored layers of fabric are basted together and designs are cut through from the top to reveal the layers beneath. The edges of the opening are turned under and invisibly hemmed. The next layers are handled in the same way.

This elegant floral quilt uses an unusual color scheme of vermilion, pink, and yellow. The linear arrangement of the floral motifs with the vertical run of diamonds gives the quilt a strong sense of movement.

Summary Berries

1860
Pennsylvania, USA
188 x 203.2 cm / 74 x 80 in
PRIVATE COLLECTION

 Floral appliqué quilts are usually valued for their realistic representation and their fine needlework.

This cornucopia of summer berries sweeps into a secondary design of interlocking circles and four-pointed stars. Once the eye has established the circles, it is hard to read the quilt as clusters of berries. The strength of the geometric illusion has subdued the imagery to a secondary role.

The quilt has been beautifully appliquéed and the plump appearance of the berries has been achieved using a technique called trapunto. Also called Italian quilting, it is a method of quilting in which double rows of stitching form pockets, which are filled from the back of the quilt with cotton batting.

Patriotic Crazy Quilt

twentieth century
USA
172 x 142 cm / 68 x 56 in
PRIVATE COLLECTION

From a distance this highly decorative quilt top looks like a tablet of hieroglyphics from a lost civilization. On a foundation of black woolen cloth the maker has created a fascinating network of interlocking shapes. Using colorful silk threads she has freely embroidered the throw with an intricate topstitch. The improvisational quality of the embroidery is harnessed by dividing bands of silk ribbon.

Crazy work was not exclusively the domain of quilts. The delicacy of these pieces made them more suitable as decorative throws, screens, curtains, tea cosies and mantlepiece scarves.

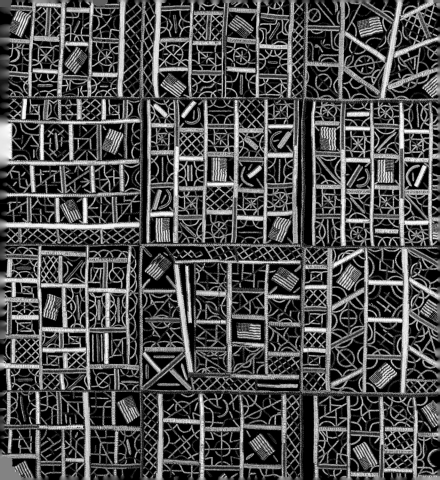

Album Coverlet

c. 1850

New York State, USA

193 x 218 cm / 76 x 86 in

COURTESY MARTHA JACKSON COLLECTION

This lovely mid-nineteenth-century appliqué coverlet, filled with motifs associated with marriage such as the *Rose of Sharon* and the *Rose Wreath*, suggest that is was made as a wedding gift. The initials of the bride and groom are pieced in each corner—a characteristic of nineteenth-century quilts from the New York, New Jersey, and Connecticut areas. The sinuous and leafy quality of the appliquéed vine that follows the borders and sashing is echoed in the choice and expression of the delicate appliqué of the blocks.

Centennial Album Quilt

c. 1776-1880

North Adams, Massachusetts, USA

199.4 x 201.3 cm / 78 1/2 x 79 1/4 in

SHELBURNE MUSEUM, VERMONT, USA

 This detailed appliqué is a testament to the excitement brought about by the 100-year anniversary of the United States. Even without the direct statements towards the Centennial such as "Declaration of Independence", it is easy to conjure feelings of patriotism.

Using various images of architecture, art, and pastimes, this quilt gives us a wonderful insight into Victorian domestic life.

Oakleaf and Reel
Presentation Quilt

c. 1850

Pennsylvania, USA

257 x 257 cm / 101 x 101 in

PRIVATE COLLECTION

This handsome quilt is an individual interpretation of the traditional *Oakleaf and Reel* pattern. It carries a personal inscription, beautifully written in indelible ink on the central block—"A Donation to the Rev John Farquhar from the Ladies of the Chanceford Congregation".

Paradise Tree Appliqué

c. 1930

Pennsylvania, USA

203 x 218 cm / 80 x 86 in

PRIVATE COLLECTION

This lovely delicately colored quilt recalls Elizabethan crewel embroidery and the central tree design is reminiscent of the colorful Indian printed cottons that frequently featured the "Tree of Life" motif. We believe this pattern was issued as a quilt kit which would have supplied the maker with some or all of the required materials.

Red and Green Floral Appliqué

c. 1850

Pennsylvania, USA

218 x 218 cm / 86 x 86 in

PRIVATE COLLECTION

This cheerful red and green appliqué quilt was made before the American Civil War. The maker has used symbolic motifs that express permanence, freedom, and well-being— schoolhouses flanked by the great Charter Oak create a border around the bountiful harvest wreaths. The one-room schoolhouse is a significant American symbol. In the primitive and often dangerous New World, it came to represent stability and respectability.

Legend has it that the Charter Oak of Hartford, Connecticut was the hiding place of the Colonial Charter of Connecticut when James 11 of England demanded its surrender to the Dominion of New England.

Garden of Eden

c. 1926
Philadelphia, Pennsylvania, USA
185.4 x 205.7 cm / 73 x 81 in
COURTESY MARTHA JACKSON COLLECTION

Provenance has it that that this quilt was made as a wedding gift for the marriage of members of two prominent families from Philadelphia. It is an unusual choice of subject matter for a bridal quilt. Usually these are album type quilts appliquéed with floral and symbolic motifs of union and happiness. This quilt depicts, in Hollywood style, the moment of terrible realization when Adam and Eve come to understand the significance of biting the Apple.

It has been appliquéed in the pastel colors that were so popular with quiltmakers in the early part of the twentieth century; prominent are the "Pastoral" colors of rose pink, lilac, copen blue, and Nile green.

Album Quilt

signed "Mary E. Rutland"
c. 1860
North Carolina, USA
198 x 213 cm / 78 x 84 in
PRIVATE COLLECTION

Five different hands have signed this quilt in pencil—Dellia Howell, S. Howell, Ida Weller, E. M. Rutland and Mary E. Rutland. Mary we know was an African–American woman from the Smithville district of Brunswick County, North Carolina. She has embroidered her name prominently in red thread across the chalice, which suggests that she may have been the principal maker. The Rutland quilt uses similar motifs as used by white quilters of the same period—oak leaves, wreaths, hearts, love apples, and the Rose of Sharon, but the treatment is more rugged and abstract. The inclusion of domestic images and strong religious icons reveals much about the preoccupations and social status of the makers.

Flower Baskets

c. 1940

Michigan, USA

208.3 x 208.3 cm / 82 x 82 in

PRIVATE COLLECTION

 This simple, springtime quilt has been executed in the fashionable pastel shades of the 1940s. Nine charming floral baskets, each set in a window, are framed by strips of delicate pink shirting fabric. The quilt has been playfully constructed using blocks set on point, resulting in shapes that constantly shift emphasis. Large blue diamonds vie with smaller white shapes for dominance.

Three different quilting patterns have been used to stitch the quilt layers together—cable, zigzag and cross-hatch. The appliqué details have been highlighted with a buttonhole stitch embroidered in contrasting colored thread.

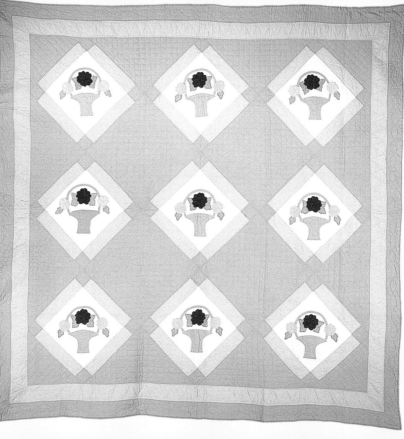

Sunflowers

c. 1912

USA

188 x 213 cm / 74 x 84 in

PRIVATE COLLECTION

This highly stylized pattern was designed by Mrs Marie Webster, needlework editor of *Ladies Home Journal* when it was one of the most popular and influential women's magazines in the United States at the turn of the century. Mrs Webster was also the author of the first serious book devoted to the history of the American quilt entitled *Quilts, Their Story and How to Make Them*, published in 1926.

Cowboy Quilt

c. 1940s

USA

218.4 x 167.6 cm / 86 x 66 in

COURTESY GIDEON WEIL

 Possibly derived from a 1940s quilt kit, this design has been painstakingly personalized with detailed and elaborate embroidery. Distinctive quilting radiates in a sunburst pattern from the center, and there is a fine feathered border around the beautifully scalloped edge. The rather inspired central motif bears a strong resemblance to earlier central medallion styles, the colors of the appliquéed figures having been carefully chosen to give a three-dimensional quality to the scene.

Love Apple

c. 1870
Pennsylvania, USA
213 x 193 cm / 84 x 76 in
PRIVATE COLLECTION

The love apple is more familiarly known as the tomato, which, at the time that this quilt was made, was prized by gardeners and considered to be an aphrodisiac. The regularly placed fruits on their vine are framed by an intricate chrome yellow, pink, and green diamond border.

Shooting Stars

c. 1920
Missouri, USA
182.9 x 193 cm / 72 x 76in
PRIVATE COLLECTION

This is a patriotic design that radiates with movement suggestive of firecrackers, shooting stars, and the Fourth of July celebration. The large design is a 1920s variation on the traditional *Princess Feather* pattern, using swirling Nile green motifs appliquéed onto a crisp white background.

The Old Homestead Quilt

designed by Anny Evason
made by Jenni Dobson
c. 1996
Loughborough, Leicestershire, England
210.8 x 209.6 cm / 83 x 82 in
PRIVATE COLLECTION

This large quilt boasts many features commonly associated with Folk Art quilts. There are pictoral blocks, pieced blocks, decorative filler blocks with appliqué leaves, flowers, hearts, stars and moons, all fitted together with simple strip piecing. Although the design of the quilt may appear complicated, rest assured that you can approach it in a relaxed manner, building up each component as you go along.

Rose Wreath

c. 1881
USA
198.1 x 243.8 cm / 78 x 96 in
PRIVATE COLLECTION

The delicate quilting of an all-over heart pattern suggests that this colorful bedcover may have been made to celebrate a wedding. It has been expertly appliquéed with motifs in bright shades of red and blue with chrome orange accents that are cleverly echoed in the decorative border.

Birds in Baskets

1870

Pennsylvania, USA

203.2 x 203.2 cm / 80 x 80 in

PRIVATE COLLECTION

 The theme of birds and baskets, both of which appear in Colonial American chintz, broderie perse, and medallion quilts as early as the mid-eighteenth century, have been delightfully interpreted in this unusual and delicate quilt.

Bluebird

1952

Tennessee, USA

210.8 x 210.8 cm / 83 x 83 in

PRIVATE COLLECTION

 Made in Tennessee in 1952, this delightful
quilt has the innocence and charm of a
rustic quilt. The large template pieces and
smooth curves make this a simple quilt to appliqué.

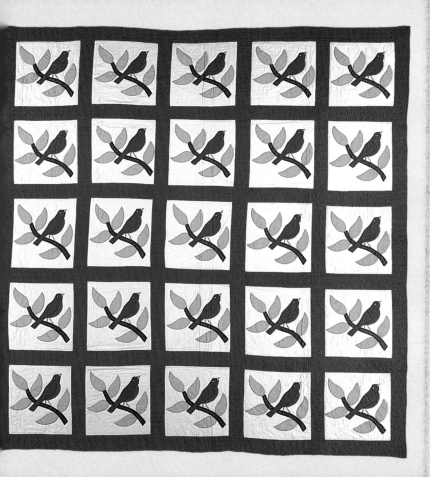

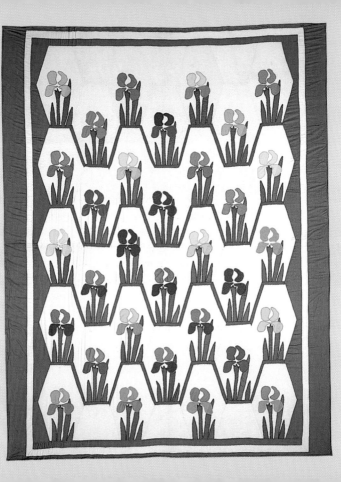

Iris

1930s

USA

244 x 198 cm / 96 x 78 in

PRIVATE COLLECTION

The six-sided, lozenge-shaped background of each block of the quilt creates a compelling setting for these colorful irises. Although the designer, Ruby Short McKim, suggested a general approach to this design, it was the maker's personal interpretation to add the charming inner green border that gracefully follows the block contour. The design is further individualized by the decorative top-stitching on the Deco-inspired petals and stems. The outer border frames of green and white are simple and crisp.

Dresden Plate

1930
St Louis, Missouri, USA
228.6 x 269.2 cm / 90 x 106 in
PRIVATE COLLECTION

 Along with *Fans* and *Grandmother's Flower Garden*, the *Dresden Plate* was one of the most popular designs of the 1920s and 1930s. Usually worked as a scrap quilt in calico prints, this variation is a celebration of rayon and acetate satin. Designed as a cheap substitute for silk that came into commercial use at the turn of the century, rayon enjoyed a short-lived popularity for making Crazy quilts, coverlets, comforters, and cushion covers.

Tulips

made by Adele Corcoran
1995
Dulwich, England
48.9 x 48.9 cm / 19 $\frac{1}{4}$ x 19 $\frac{1}{4}$ in
PRIVATE COLLECTION

Appliqué quilts reached a peak of popularity during the first half of the twentieth century. Syndicated newspaper columns reached needlewomen across the country with an enormous variety of appliqué patterns. None were more popular than flowers, and they appeared in all styles and degrees of sophistication.

The "municipal" green, a hallmark of British public buildings in the 1920s and 1930s, became a part of the quilter's palette of the period and provides a wonderful counterpoint for the bright colors of the tulips.

211

The Lennox Quilt

signed and dated "Martha Lennox, 1712"
Ireland
182.9 x 198.1 cm / 72 x 78 in

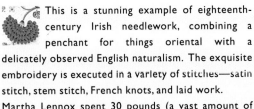This is a stunning example of eighteenth-century Irish needlework, combining a penchant for things oriental with a delicately observed English naturalism. The exquisite embroidery is executed in a variety of stitches—satin stitch, stem stitch, French knots, and laid work.

Martha Lennox spent 30 pounds (a vast amount of money in the eighteenth century) on French embroidery silk to complete this brilliantly colored and stitched heirloom piece. Through her skilled use of colors, sometimes combining three or four shades of one color, she achieves a rich painterly effect.

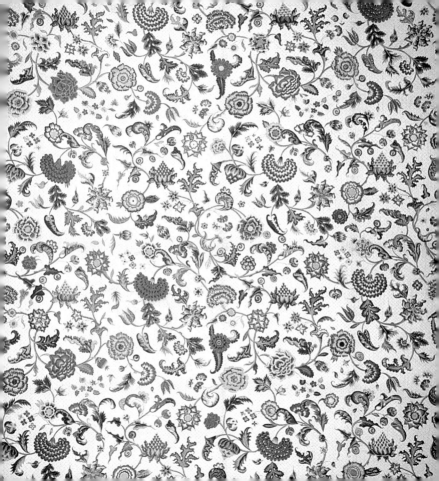

Spring Bouquet

1930
USA
223.5 x 264.2 cm / 88 x 104 in
PRIVATE COLLECTION

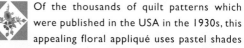 Of the thousands of quilt patterns which were published in the USA in the 1930s, this appealing floral appliqué uses pastel shades which were fashionable between the wars.

Cat by the Summer House

designed and made by Janet Bolton
1997
London, England
20.32 x 24.13 cm / 8 x 9¹/₂ in
PRIVATE COLLECTION

 A summer house is often an excuse for a flight of fancy; a delicious structure hidden in some far away corner of a garden. A summer house is frequently built from all sorts of collected materials, and offers a way in which an inventive person can satisfy the longing for self-sufficiency.

Cat by the Summer House, uses a mixture of old and new fabrics as well as hand dyed prints to create the soft sunbleached look of summer.

Sampler Quilt

made by Mamie Drukenbrod
1895
Schoneck, Pennsylvania, USA
298.1 x 223.5 cm / 78 x 88 in
COURTESY ALY GOODWIN

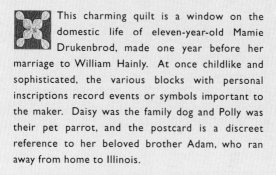 This charming quilt is a window on the domestic life of eleven-year-old Mamie Drukenbrod, made one year before her marriage to William Hainly. At once childlike and sophisticated, the various blocks with personal inscriptions record events or symbols important to the maker. Daisy was the family dog and Polly was their pet parrot, and the postcard is a discreet reference to her beloved brother Adam, who ran away from home to Illinois.

Princess Feather

nineteenth century
New England, USA
193 x 188 cm / 76 x 74 in
PRIVATE COLLECTION

The *Princess Feather* quilt, particularly set out in fashionable reds, greens, and yellows, enjoyed enormous popularity during the nineteenth century. This fascinating example has an added imperial flourish of beautiful stuffed work (trapunto) in both the vine border and center nlne blocks.

Mola Quilt

made by Ann Tuck
1998
Newcastle-upon-Tyne, England
94 x 94 cm / 37 x 37 in

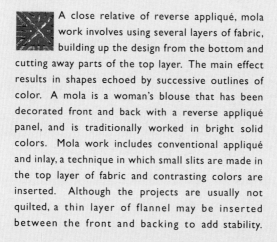 A close relative of reverse appliqué, mola work involves using several layers of fabric, building up the design from the bottom and cutting away parts of the top layer. The main effect results in shapes echoed by successive outlines of color. A mola is a woman's blouse that has been decorated front and back with a reverse appliqué panel, and is traditionally worked in bright solid colors. Mola work includes conventional appliqué and inlay, a technique in which small slits are made in the top layer of fabric and contrasting colors are inserted. Although the projects are usually not quilted, a thin layer of flannel may be inserted between the front and backing to add stability.

Rabbit Patch Quilt

made by Ngarie Brook
1998
Orewa, New Zealand
97.2 x 105.4 cm / 38 x 41 in
PRIVATE COLLECTION

 This charming wallhanging, with its stylized floral motifs, twisted vines, and well-dressed rabbit, is ideal for experienced stitchers who enjoy three-dimensional work and novelty work. It relies for its appeal on hand appliqué, yo-yos, and button embellishments.

Ohio Rose Appliqué

1930
USA
157.5 x 203.2 cm / 62 x 80 in
PRIVATE COLLECTION

Subtle shades of green and pink with pale yellow and bright red accents on a cream ground help bring this beautiful quilt to life. There is exceptional echo quilting around the twelve appliqué blocks with feathers, while the surrounding vine border helps complete its charm.

Flowerpot Appliqué

made by Adele Corcoran
1995
Dulwich, England
91.4 x 91.4 cm / 36 x 36 in
PRIVATE COLLECTION

No windowsill is ever complete without an arrangement full of plants. And none was ever more orderly than these cheerful, perpetually blooming pots. They prove that the simplest flower shapes can not only provide easy patterns, but endless pleasure as well.

Inspired by a 1930s quilt, this small wallhanging takes its particular charm from a rich array of period fabrics and the innovative treatment of the stems.

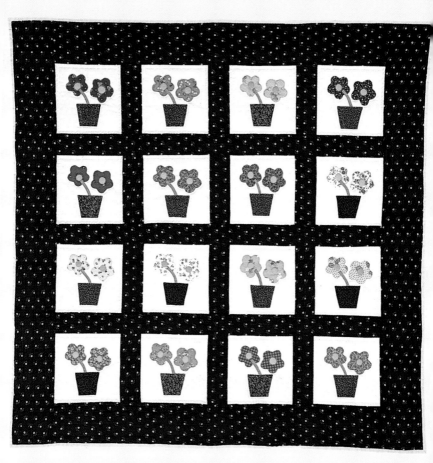

Story Quilt

made by Mary Clare Clark
1995
London, England
182.9 x 137.2 cm / 72 x 54 in
PRIVATE COLLECTION

Each one of the panels within this quilt was inspired by a pictorial quilt from the last century, and each one considers a focal needlework technique to explore. The twelve panels can be made individually as wallhangings, or incorporated into one single quilt as shown here. It is easy to admire the vibrant colors and non-stop action of a story quilt that chronicles the hardships of settling the west to the story of Adam and Eve in the Garden of Eden.

Thistle Appliqué

1860
Pennsylvania, USA
203.2 x 233.7 cm / 80 x 92 in
PRIVATE COLLECTION

This charming piece is typical of the American penchant for red, white, and green quilts, a style favored by German immigrants in Pennsylvania. Appliqué patterns from the middle of the last century often featured swag borders and a variety of bows, hearts, and flower motifs. The generous dimensions of this quilt reflect the use of large family beds which were in vogue prior to the American Civil War in 1862.

Appliqué Bedcover

made by Sarah Furman Warner
c. 1800
Greenfield Hill, Connecticut, USA
266.7 x 213.4 cm / 105 x 84 in
HENRY FORD MUSEUM

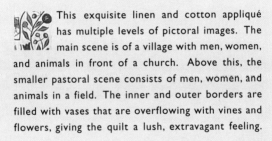 This exquisite linen and cotton appliqué has multiple levels of pictoral images. The main scene is of a village with men, women, and animals in front of a church. Above this, the smaller pastoral scene consists of men, women, and animals in a field. The inner and outer borders are filled with vases that are overflowing with vines and flowers, giving the quilt a lush, extravagant feeling.

Sunbonnet Sue

1930
Missouri, USA
172.7 x 213.4 cm / 68 x 84 in

A nostalgic design popularized in the 1930s, this is one of the thousands of patterns that was commercially distributed throughout the United States. The silhouetted image of Sue bears a remarkable similarity to early Kate Greenaway drawings and Dutch engravings. The sentimental motif may have been appropriated by twentieth-century quilters to satisfy a longing for simplicity and a return to traditional rural values.

Blue and White Hawaiian

c. 1930

Hawaii, USA

203.2 x 246.4 cm / 80 x 97 in

COURTESY JOHN R. SAULS, TYLER, TEXAS

Introduced to quilting in the nineteenth century by visiting missionaries, the Hawaiians rapidly developed their own distinctive appliqué style derived from folded cut-paper designs. The work is distinguished by the use of bold and abstract styles of one, usually dark, color cut from a single piece of fabric which is set against a white ground. The designs frequently draw inspiration from Hawaii's exotic flora.

Welsh Pictorial Quilt

made by James Williams
1852
Wrexham, Clwyd, Wales
208.3 x 228.6 cm / 82 x 90 in
COURTESY THE MUSEUM OF WELSH LIFE,
ST FAGANS, WALES

 This exciting textile picture was made by tailor James Williams over a period of ten years, using a technique of inlay. It is a form of appliqué in which the shapes and patterns are cut from the main fabric and replaced by different colored fabrics. The work is a marvelous design of pictorial detail and abstract geometric patterns. The picture is composed asymmetrically, reminiscent of the way in which a crazy quilt is constructed. Using a dazzling array of colorful regimental facing cloths and felted cloth, Williams has created a wealth of different geometric border patterns to envelop a number of Biblical stories.

Antrim Bed Furniture

eighteenth century
Ireland
152.4 x 157.5 cm / 60 x 62 in
COURTESY THE TRUSTEES OF THE NATIONAL
MUSEUMS AND GALLERIES OF
NORTHERN IRELAND

 Quilting in the early part of the eighteenth century was considered as a kind of embroidery, and in this coverlet the two disciplines work together beautifully. It was made by, or under the instruction of, Lady Helena McDonnel (1705–1783), sister of the 5th Earl of Antrim.

On a canvas of ivory silk an elaborate floral medallion with an unusual garland border has been embroidered in a variety of stitches. It has been executed with such skill as to appear three-dimensional, with the leaves achieving a rich velvety depth. The background has been densely stitched in gold thread, in an overall vermicular pattern.

Scottie Dogs

c. 1930

Indiana, USA

280.7 x 231.1 cm / 79 x 91 in

COURTESY JOHN R. SAULS, TYLER, TEXAS

 Contemporary events inspired commercial pattern houses to create a catalog of new and often light-hearted quilt patterns. The Roosevelt presidency was commemorated with a Roosevelt Rose, eagle designs symbolized the National Recovery Act and the Scottie dog became a celebrated quilt motif after Roosevelt's speech about his little dog Fala.

Folk Art Marriage Quilt

1860
Pennsylvania, USA
188 x 213.4 cm / 74 x 84 in
PRIVATE COLLECTION

This early Pennsylvania quilt has a delightful folk quality. It has been made with exquisite precision but has the light-hearted idiosyncracies that gives it its distinctive quality. The flowing swag and tasseled border, resembling wedding bells, is punctuated with more hearts in the corners.

Cupid's Heart

made by Linda M. Roy
1992
Conway, Arkansas, USA
208.7 x 205.7 cm / 81 x 81 in
COURTESY INTERNATIONAL QUILT FESTIVAL,
HOUSTON, TEXAS

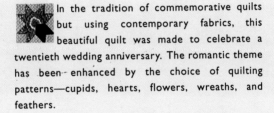In the tradition of commemorative quilts but using contemporary fabrics, this beautiful quilt was made to celebrate a twentieth wedding anniversary. The romantic theme has been enhanced by the choice of quilting patterns—cupids, hearts, flowers, wreaths, and feathers.

Palampore

c. 1853

India

330.2 x 264.2 cm / 130 x 104 in

COURTESY SARAH FRANKLYN, LONDON,
ENGLAND

The word palampore refers to a painted, dyed and glazed cotton bedcover made in India and imported into England during the late seventeenth and eighteenth centuries. Europe was entranced by the brilliant and exotic appearance of this new printed textile. Chintz, to the detriment of all other European textiles, became the foremost dress and furnishing fabric for almost a hundred years.

This palampore was made for the Great Exhibition in Paris in 1885. The design is of a central, flowering tree on a single chintz panel. Stylistically, it is a late example of this type of bedcover and features many Western preferences, especially obvious in the use of heavy swag borders and bows.

Acknowledgments

p129 photographic reproduction courtesy of the Quilters' Guild of the British Isles; p141, p239, p244 photographic reproduction courtesy of John R. Sauls, Texas; p143 courtesy of Ron Simpson; p159 photographic reproduction courtesy of Betsy Nimock; p160 courtesy of Victoria Weil; p175 and p185 photographic reproduction courtesy of Martha Jackson; p176 photographic reproduction courtesy of The Shelburne Museum, Vermont; p193 courtesy of Gideon Weil; p212 and p243 photographs reproduced courtesy of the Trustees of the National Museums & Galleries of Northern Ireland; p219 photographic reproduction courtesy of Aly Goodwin; p235 photographic reproduction courtesy of the Henry Ford Museum, Michigan; p240 photographic reproduction courtesy of the Museum of Welsh Life, St Fagans, Wales; p249 photographic reproduction courtesy of the International Quilt Festival Houston, Texas; p251 photographic reproduction courtesy of Sarah Franklyn, London, England

Index

16-Patch on Point 84
Album Coverlet 175
Album Quilt 152
Album Quilt 187
Alphabet Quilt 148
Amish Bars 92
Amish Bear's Paw 34
Amish Broken Star 134
Amish Crown of Thorns 45
Amish Diamond in a Square 18

Amish Log Cabin, Barn Raising Variation 65
Amish Lone Star 131
Amish Nine-patch 29
Amish Sunshine and Shadow 100
Amish Unknown Design 80
Anne Price 7
Antrim Bed Furniture 242

Appliqué Bedcover 234
Basket with Eight-point Star 14
Birds in Basket 203
Birds in the Air 115
Black and White Optical Illusion 136
Blue and White Hawaiian 238
Bluebird 204

Carpenter's Square 99

Cat by the Summer House 216

Centennial Album Quilt 176

Centennial Eagle 151

Charles Lindburgh Commemorative 38

Churn Dash 138

Cowboy Quilt 192

Coxcomb and Currant Variation 147

Cupid's Heart 248

Double Irish Chain 116

Double Wedding Ring 75

Dove at the Window 30

Dresden Plate 208

Drunkard's Path 119

Early Nine-patch 22

Evergreen 68

Feathered Star in Blue and Gold 83

Figurative Crazy Quilt 159

Flags 141

Floral Reverse Appliqué 168

Flower Baskets 188

Flowerpot Appliqué 228

Flowerpots 58

Flying Geese 91

Folk Art Marriage Quilt 246

Garden of Eden 184

Grandmother's Flower Garden 54

Iris 207

Jane Austen Quilt 127

Lennox Quilt, The 212

Log Cabin, Hap Quilt 124

Log Cabin, Light and Dark
   Variation 57
Log Cabin, Pineapple
   Variation 49
Lone Star 142
Love and Luck 156
Love Apple 195

Mammy Quilt 164
Maple Leaf 104
Mariner's Compass 17
Medallion Sampler 41
Mennonite Baskets 79
Mennonite Joseph's Coat
   33

Mennonite Log Cabin -
   123
Mennonite Starburst 95
Military Patchwork 53
Missouri Folk Art Lily 120
Mola Quilt 223

New York Beauty 10, 61
North Carolina Lily 87

Oakleaf and Reel
   Presentation Quilt 179
Ocean Waves 21
Ohio Rose Appliqué 227
Ohio Star 76

Old Homestead Quilt, The
   199

Palampore 250
Paradise Tree Appliqué 180
Patriotic Crazy Quilt 172
Pennsylvania Dutch Folk
   Art Appliqué 167
Pennsylvania Wreath 2
Poppyfield II 128
Prairie Stars with Prairie
   Points 108
Primitive Schoolhouses
   72
Princess Feather 220

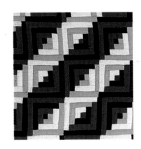

Princess Feather Variation 163
Pyramids 111

Rabbit Patch Quilt 224
Rainbow Schoolhouses 96
Red and Green Floral Appliqué 183
Rose Wreath 200

Sailors 155
Sampler Quilt 219
Scottie Dogs 245
Seven Sisters 88
Shoo-fly 42

Shooting Stars 196
Silk Tumbling Blocks 62
Snow Crystals 112
Spools 50
Spring Bouquet 215
Stars 25
Story Quilt 231
String of Flags 103
Summer Berries 171
Sunbonnet Sue 236
Sunflowers 191

Thistle Appliqué 232
Tree of Life 37
Tulips 211

Underground Railroad 26
Union Army Encircled Star 133

Victorian Crazy Crib Quilt 71
Welsh Pictorial Quilt 241
Whig's Defeat 160

Young Man's Fancy 46
Yo-yo Quilt 66

Zigzag Bricks 107